The Vibrant Beet Cookbook

Discover the Nutritional Benefits and Versatile Uses of Beets in Your Cooking with 100 Mouth-Watering Recipes for Every Occasion

Timothy Parker

TABLE OF CONTENTS

INTRODUCTION

Are you looking for a new ingredient to add to your kitchen repertoire? Look no further than the humble beet! Often overlooked in the produce aisle, beets are a root vegetable that are packed with nutrients, from vitamins and minerals to antioxidants and nitrates.

But beets aren't just good for you – they're also incredibly versatile in the kitchen. From roasted beet salads to beet hummus, beet burgers, and even beet brownies, there are endless ways to incorporate beets into your cooking. Plus, their vibrant color adds a beautiful pop to any dish.

In this cookbook, we'll be sharing 100 mouth-watering recipes that showcase the versatility and nutritional benefits of beets. Whether you're a seasoned beet lover or new to this root vegetable, we've got recipes for every occasion, from hearty mains to refreshing sides and sweet treats.

We'll also be sharing some of our best tips and techniques for cooking with beets, so you can get the most out of this delicious and nutritious ingredient. So, grab a copy of this cookbook and start exploring the world of beets – your taste buds (and your body) will thank you!

BREAKFAST

1. Bowl of raspberry and almond milk

Makes: 3

INGREDIENTS:
- 1 cup frozen raspberries
- ¼ cup collagen peptides
- ¼ cup MCT oil
- 2 tablespoons of chia seeds
- 1 teaspoon beetroot powder
- 1 teaspoon organic vanilla extract
- 4 drops of liquid stevia
- 1 ½ cup almond milk, unsweetened

INSTRUCTIONS:
a) In a high-powered blender, combine all ingredients and blend until smooth.
b) Pour into 3 serving bowls and serve with your favorite garnish.

2. Pink Pickled Eggs

Makes: 6

INGREDIENTS:
- 6 eggs
- 1 cup white vinegar
- Juice from 1 can of beets
- ¼ cup sugar
- ½ tablespoon salt
- 2 cloves garlic
- 1 tablespoon whole peppercorn
- 1 bay leaf

INSTRUCTIONS:

a) Preheat the water bath to 170 °F.

b) Place eggs in a bag. Seal the bag and place it in the bath. Cook for 1 hour.

c) After 1 hour, place eggs in a bowl of cold water to cool and carefully peel. In the bag in which you cooked the eggs, combine vinegar, beet juice, sugar, salt, garlic, and bay leaf.

d) Replace eggs in a bag with pickling liquid. Replace in a water bath and cook for 1 additional hour.

e) After 1 hour, move eggs with pickling liquid to a refrigerator.

f) Allow cooling completely before eating.

3. Beet latkes

Makes: 1 Serving

INGREDIENTS:

- 1 cup Finely chopped fresh beets
- 2 tablespoons Cornstarch
- 4 Egg yolks beaten
- ½ teaspoon Sugar
- 3 tablespoons Heavy cream or undiluted evaporated milk
- ½ teaspoon Ground nutmeg
- 1 teaspoon Salt

INSTRUCTIONS:

a) Combine all ingredients in a mixing bowl.

b) Mix well and bake in pancake fashion on a hot buttered griddle or heavy skillet.

c) Serve with Fruit marmalade or preserves.

4. Lancaster beets & eggs

Makes: 1 Batch

INGREDIENTS:
- 16 ounces Beets, sliced canned
- ¾ cup Cider vinegar
- 6 tablespoons Sugar, granulated
- 1 tablespoon Pickling spice
- 1 small Onion; cut into rings
- ½ cup; Water, hot
- 4 Egg; hard-cooked, shelled
- 3 tablespoons Mayonnaise
- 1 teaspoon Mustard, prepared
- ⅛ teaspoon Salt

INSTRUCTIONS

a) Drain liquid from beets into a medium saucepan. Stir in vinegar, sugar, and pickling spices. Heat to boiling, and simmer for five minutes.

b) Strain into a two-cup measure.

c) Combine beets and onion in a medium bowl; add one cup of the pickling liquid; stir to mix; chill.

d) Stir hot water into the remaining pickling liquid; pour over eggs in a medium bowl. Let stand, turning several times, for about an hour or until eggs are a rich pink; drain off the liquid. Chill eggs until ready to stuff.

e) Halve eggs lengthwise; scoop out yolks into a small bowl; mash well.

f) Beat in salad dressing, mustard, and salt until the mixture is light and fluffy. Pile back into whites.

g) Drain liquid from beets and onions; spoon into the center of a serving dish. Place devilled eggs in a ring around the edge.

5. Skillet Beets, Spinach, and Eggs

Makes: 2

INGREDIENTS

- 2 small beets of red and gold
- 2 eggs
- 1 cup spinach
- 1 tablespoon coconut oil
- 1 teaspoon basil
- ¼ teaspoon pepper
- ¼ teaspoon sea salt

INSTRUCTIONS

a) Peel the beets then chop them into small pieces. Sauté with coconut oil, herbs, and seasoning in a skillet until they start to soften up.

b) Push the beets to the side of the skillet and crack the eggs in. Cook for a minute or two, depending on how you like them. While they finish cooking toss some spinach in to heat up on a separate side of the pan.

c) Once everything is ready remove from heat and serve warm!

6. Beet Hash with Eggs

Makes: 4

INGREDIENTS:
- 1 pound beets, peeled and diced
- ½ pound Yukon Gold potatoes, scrubbed and diced
- Coarse salt and freshly ground black pepper
- 2 tablespoons extra-virgin olive oil
- 1 small onion, diced
- 2 tablespoons chopped fresh parsley
- 4 large eggs

INSTRUCTIONS:

a) In a high-sided skillet, cover beets and potatoes with water and bring to a boil. Season with salt and cook until tender, about 7 minutes. Drain and wipe out the skillet.

b) Heat oil in a skillet over medium-high heat. Add boiled beets and potatoes and cook until potatoes begin to turn golden about 4 minutes. Reduce heat to medium, add onion, and cook, stirring, until tender, about 4 minutes. Adjust seasoning and stir in parsley.

c) Make four wide wells in the hash. Crack one egg into each and season the egg with salt. Cook until whites set but yolks are still runny 5 to 6 minutes.

7. Beet Crust Breakfast Pizza

Makes: 6

INGREDIENTS:
FOR THE PIZZA CRUST:
- 1 cup boiled and pureed beets
- ¾ cup almond meal
- ⅓ cup brown rice flour
- ½ teaspoon salt
- 2 teaspoons baking powder
- 1 tablespoon coconut oil
- 2 teaspoons rosemary chopped up
- 1 egg

TOPPINGS:
- 3 Eggs
- 2 slices of cooked bacon crumbled up
- avocado
- cheese

INSTRUCTIONS
a) Preheat oven to 375 degrees
b) Mix all the ingredients for the pizza crust
c) Bake for 5 minutes
d) Take out and make 3 small "wells" using the back of a spoon or ice cream mold
e) Drop the 3 eggs into these "wells"
f) Bake 20 minutes
g) Top with cheese and bacon and bake for 5 more minutes
h) Add more rosemary, cheese, and avocado.

8. Beet and Goat Cheese Frittata

Ingredients:

1 large beet, peeled and grated
6 large eggs
1/4 cup crumbled goat cheese
1 tbsp olive oil
1/4 tsp salt
1/4 tsp black pepper
1/4 cup chopped fresh parsley
Instructions:

Preheat the oven to 350°F.

In a large mixing bowl, whisk together the eggs, goat cheese, grated beet, salt, and pepper.

Heat the olive oil in a large oven-safe skillet over medium heat.

Pour the egg mixture into the skillet and cook for 2-3 minutes, until the bottom is set.

Transfer the skillet to the oven and bake for 8-10 minutes, until the frittata is cooked through.

Sprinkle with chopped parsley and serve.

9. Beet and Berry Smoothie Bowl

Ingredients:

1 large beet, peeled and diced
1 cup frozen mixed berries
1 banana
1/2 cup almond milk
1 tbsp honey
1 tsp vanilla extract
1/4 cup granola
1 tbsp chia seeds
Instructions:

Add the diced beet, frozen berries, banana, almond milk, honey, and vanilla extract to a blender.

Blend until smooth and creamy.

Pour the smoothie into a bowl.

Top with granola and chia seeds.

Serve immediately.

10. Beet and Sweet Potato Hash

Ingredients:

1 large beet, peeled and diced
1 large sweet potato, peeled and diced
1 onion, diced
2 cloves garlic, minced
2 tbsp olive oil
1/2 tsp salt
1/4 tsp black pepper
4 eggs
Instructions:

Heat the olive oil in a large skillet over medium heat.

Add the diced beet, sweet potato, onion, and garlic to the skillet.

Cook for 15-20 minutes, stirring occasionally, until the vegetables are tender.

Season with salt and pepper.

Crack the eggs into the skillet and cook for 2-3 minutes, until the whites are set and the yolks are still runny.

Serve immediately.

11. Beet and Avocado Toast

Ingredients:

1 large beet, peeled and grated
2 slices whole wheat bread
1 avocado, sliced
1/4 tsp salt
1/4 tsp black pepper
1 tbsp olive oil
1 tbsp chopped fresh cilantro

Instructions:

Toast the slices of bread.

In a small mixing bowl, combine the grated beet, salt, black pepper, and olive oil.

Spread the beet mixture onto the toast.

Top with sliced avocado.

Sprinkle with chopped cilantro.

Serve immediately.

12. Beet and Yogurt Parfait

Ingredients:

1 large beet, peeled and grated
1 cup Greek yogurt
1 tbsp honey
1/2 cup granola
1/4 cup mixed berries (optional)
Instructions:

In a small mixing bowl, combine the grated beet, Greek yogurt, and honey.
Layer the yogurt mixture and granola in a glass.
Top with mixed berries, if desired.
Serve immediately.

13. Beet and Carrot Breakfast Tacos

Ingredients:

1 large beet, peeled and grated
1 large carrot, peeled and grated
4 small corn tortillas
4 eggs
1/4 tsp salt
1/4 tsp black pepper
2 tbsp olive oil
1 tbsp chopped fresh cilantro
Instructions:

Heat the olive oil in a large skillet over medium heat.

Add the grated beet and carrot to the skillet.

Cook for 10-15 minutes, stirring occasionally, until the vegetables are tender.

Season with salt and pepper.

In a separate skillet, fry the eggs until the whites are set and the yolks are still runny.

Warm the tortillas in the oven or microwave.

Assemble the tacos by filling each tortilla with the beet and carrot mixture and a fried egg.

Top with chopped cilantro.

Serve immediately.

14. Beet and Ricotta Toast with Balsamic Glaze

Ingredients:

1 large beet, peeled and grated
2 slices whole wheat bread
1/2 cup ricotta cheese
1 tbsp balsamic glaze
1 tbsp chopped fresh basil
Instructions:

Toast the slices of bread.

Spread the ricotta cheese onto the toast.

Top with the grated beet.

Drizzle the balsamic glaze over the beet.

Sprinkle with chopped basil.

Serve immediately.

15. Beet and Quinoa Breakfast Bowl

Ingredients:

1 large beet, peeled and diced
1 cup cooked quinoa
1/2 cup chopped kale
1/4 cup crumbled feta cheese
1 tbsp olive oil
1/4 tsp salt
1/4 tsp black pepper
1 tbsp chopped fresh parsley
Instructions:

Heat the olive oil in a large skillet over medium heat.

Add the diced beet to the skillet and cook for 10-15 minutes, stirring occasionally, until the beet is tender.

Add the chopped kale to the skillet and cook for an additional 2-3 minutes, until the kale is wilted.

Season with salt and pepper.

In a mixing bowl, combine the cooked quinoa, beet mixture, and crumbled feta cheese.

Divide the quinoa mixture into bowls.

Top with chopped parsley.

Serve immediately.

16. Beet and Chocolate Chia Pudding

Ingredients:

1 large beet, peeled and grated
1/2 cup chia seeds
2 cups almond milk
1/4 cup unsweetened cocoa powder
1/4 cup maple syrup
1 tsp vanilla extract
Instructions:

In a blender, combine the grated beet, almond milk, unsweetened cocoa powder, maple syrup, and vanilla extract.

Blend until smooth.

Pour the mixture into a mixing bowl.

Add the chia seeds and stir to combine.

Let the pudding sit for at least 30 minutes, or overnight in the refrigerator.

Serve chilled.

17. Beet and Sausage Breakfast Skillet

Ingredients:

1 large beet, peeled and diced
4 breakfast sausages, sliced
1 onion, diced
2 cloves garlic, minced
2 tbsp olive oil
1/2 tsp salt
1/4 tsp black pepper
4 eggs
Instructions:

Heat the olive oil in a large skillet over medium heat.
2. Add the diced beet, sliced sausages, diced onion, and minced garlic to the skillet.

Cook for 10-15 minutes, stirring occasionally, until the vegetables are tender and the sausage is browned.
Season with salt and pepper.
Create four wells in the skillet and crack an egg into each well.
Cover the skillet and cook for an additional 5-7 minutes, or until the eggs are cooked to your liking.
Serve immediately.

18. Beet and Goat Cheese Breakfast Tart

Ingredients:

1 pie crust, homemade or store-bought
1 large beet, peeled and thinly sliced
4 oz goat cheese, crumbled
2 eggs
1/4 cup heavy cream
1/4 tsp salt
1/4 tsp black pepper
1 tbsp chopped fresh thyme
Instructions:

Preheat the oven to 375°F.

Place the pie crust in a 9-inch tart pan and prick the bottom with a fork.

Arrange the thinly sliced beet on top of the crust.

In a mixing bowl, whisk together the eggs, heavy cream, salt, pepper, and chopped thyme.

Pour the egg mixture over the beet and spread it out evenly.

Sprinkle the crumbled goat cheese on top.

Bake for 25-30 minutes, or until the crust is golden brown and the filling is set.

Let the tart cool for a few minutes before slicing and serving.

SNACKS AND APPETIZERS

19. Beet Chips

Makes: 1

INGREDIENTS:
- 4 medium beets, rinse and sliced thin
- 1 teaspoon sea salt
- 2 tablespoons olive oil
- Hummus, for serving

INSTRUCTIONS:
a)   Preheat the air fryer to 380°F.

b)   In a large bowl, toss the beets with sea salt and olive oil until well coated.

c)   Put the beet slices into the air fryer and spread them out in a single layer.

d)   Fry for 10 minutes. Stir, then fry for an additional 10 minutes. Stir again, then fry for a final 5 to 10 minutes, or until the chips reach the desired crispiness.

e)   Serve with a favorite hummus.

20. Dill & Garlic Beets

Makes: 2 Servings

INGREDIENTS:
- 4 beets, cleaned, peeled, and sliced
- 1 garlic clove, minced
- 2 tablespoons chopped fresh dill
- ¼ teaspoon salt
- ¼ teaspoon black pepper
- 3 tablespoons olive oil

INSTRUCTIONS:
a) Preheat the air fryer to 380°F.

b) In a large bowl, mix all of the ingredients so the beets are well coated with the oil.

c) Pour the beet mixture into the air fryer basket, and roast for 15 minutes before stirring, then continue roasting for 15 minutes more.

21. Beet appetizer salad

Makes: 4 Servings

INGREDIENTS
- 2 pounds Beets
- Salt
- ½ each Spanish onion, diced
- 4 Tomatoes, skinned, seeded, and diced
- 2 tablespoons Vinegar
- 8 tablespoons Olive oil
- Black olives
- 2 each Garlic cloves, chopped
- 4 tablespoons Italian parsley, chopped
- 4 tablespoons Cilantro, chopped
- 4 mediums Potatoes, boiled
- Salt and pepper
- Hot red pepper

INSTRUCTIONS:
a) Cut off ends of beets. Wash well and cook in boiling salted water until tender. Drain and remove skins under running cold water. Dice.

b) Mix the dressing ingredients.

c) Combine beets in a salad bowl with the onion, tomato, garlic cilantro, and parsley. Pour over half the dressing, toss gently, and chill for 30 minutes. Slice the potatoes, place in a shallow bowl, and toss with the remaining dressing. Chill.

d) When ready to assemble, arrange beets, tomato, and onion in the center of a shallow bowl and arrange potatoes in a ring around them. Garnish with olives.

22. Beet boats

Makes: 6 servings

INGREDIENTS:
- 8 smalls Beets
- 10 ounces of Crab meat, canned or fresh
- 2 teaspoons Minced fresh parsley
- 1 teaspoon Lemon juice

INSTRUCTIONS:
a) Steam beets for 20-40 minutes, or until tender. Rinse with cold water, peel, and let cool. Meanwhile, mix crab meat, parsley, and lemon juice.

b) When beets are cool, halve and scoop out centers with a melon baller, or teaspoon, making a hollow. Stuff with crab mixture.

c) Serve as an appetizer, or for lunch along with stir-fried beet greens.

23. Beet fritters

Makes: 6 servings

INGREDIENTS:
- 2 cups Grated raw beets
- ¼ cup Onion, diced
- ½ cup Bread crumbs
- 1 large Egg, beaten
- ¼ teaspoon Ginger
- Salt and pepper to taste

INSTRUCTIONS:

a) Mix all ingredients. Spoon out pancake-sized portions onto a hot, oiled griddle.

b) Cook until brown, turning once.

c) Serve topped with butter, sour cream, yogurt, or any combination of these.

24. Stuffed beets

Makes: 6 servings

INGREDIENTS:
- 6 larges Beets
- 6 tablespoons Grated sharp cheese
- 2 tablespoons Bread crumbs
- 2 tablespoons Sour cream
- 1 tablespoon Pickle relish
- ½ teaspoon Salt
- ¼ teaspoon Pepper
- ¼ cup Butter
- ¼ cup White wine

INSTRUCTIONS:
a) Hollow out beets, or use beets that have been used for making candy cane garnishes.

b) Cook the hollowed-out beets in lightly salted water until tender.

c) Cool and remove the skins. Heat oven to 350F. Mix the cheese, bread crumbs, sour cream, pickle relish, and seasonings.

d) Stuff the beets with this mixture and place them in a shallow greased baking dish. Brush with butter and bake uncovered in a 350 F oven for 15 to 20 minutes.

e) Melt the butter and mix it with the white wine and baste occasionally to keep moist.

25. Roasted Beet Hummus

Ingredients:

1 large beet, roasted and peeled
1 can chickpeas, drained and rinsed
1/4 cup tahini
1/4 cup lemon juice
2 cloves garlic, minced
1/4 cup olive oil
Salt and pepper, to taste
Instructions:

In a food processor, pulse the roasted beet until it's finely chopped.

Add the chickpeas, tahini, lemon juice, and minced garlic.

Pulse until everything is combined.

While the food processor is running, slowly drizzle in the olive oil.

Season with salt and pepper, to taste.

Serve with pita chips or vegetables for dipping.

26. Beet and Goat Cheese Crostini

Ingredients:

1 French baguette, sliced
1 large beet, roasted and sliced
2 oz goat cheese
1 tbsp honey
1 tbsp chopped fresh thyme
Instructions:

Preheat the oven to 375°F.

Arrange the baguette slices on a baking sheet and toast in the oven for 5-7 minutes, or until they're lightly golden brown.

Spread the goat cheese onto each toast.

Layer the roasted beet on top.

Drizzle honey over the beet slices.

Sprinkle with chopped thyme.

Serve immediately.

27. Beet and Feta Dip

Ingredients:

1 large beet, roasted and peeled
4 oz feta cheese, crumbled
1/4 cup Greek yogurt
1 tbsp lemon juice
2 cloves garlic, minced
2 tbsp olive oil
Salt and pepper, to taste

Instructions:

In a food processor, pulse the roasted beet until it's finely chopped.

Add the crumbled feta cheese, Greek yogurt, lemon juice, and minced garlic.

Pulse until everything is combined.

While the food processor is running, slowly drizzle in the olive oil.

Season with salt and pepper, to taste.

Serve with pita chips or vegetables for dipping.

28. Beet and Avocado Tartare

Ingredients:

1 large beet, peeled and finely diced
1 avocado, peeled and finely diced
1/4 cup chopped fresh parsley
2 tbsp olive oil
1 tbsp lemon juice
Salt and pepper, to taste
Instructions:

In a mixing bowl, combine the diced beet, diced avocado, and chopped parsley.

Drizzle the olive oil and lemon juice over the mixture.

Season with salt and pepper, to taste.

Gently stir everything together.

Serve immediately.

29. Beet and Carrot Fritters

Ingredients:

2 medium beets, grated
2 medium carrots, grated
1/2 onion, finely chopped
1/4 cup flour
1/4 cup breadcrumbs
1 egg, beaten
2 tbsp olive oil
Salt and pepper, to taste
Instructions:

In a mixing bowl, combine the grated beets, grated carrots, finely chopped onion, flour, breadcrumbs, and beaten egg.

Season with salt and pepper, to taste.

Mix everything together until well combined.

Heat olive oil in a large skillet over medium heat.

Using a spoon or cookie scoop, drop small portions of the mixture into the hot skillet.

Fry until golden brown on both sides, about 2-3 minutes per side.

Drain on a paper towel and serve warm.

30. Beet and Apple Salad

Ingredients:

2 large beets, roasted and diced
2 medium apples, diced
1/4 cup chopped walnuts
1/4 cup crumbled blue cheese
2 tbsp olive oil
1 tbsp honey
1 tbsp apple cider vinegar
Salt and pepper, to taste
Instructions:

In a mixing bowl, combine the roasted and diced beets, diced apples, chopped walnuts, and crumbled blue cheese.

In a separate small mixing bowl, whisk together the olive oil, honey, apple cider vinegar, salt, and pepper.

Pour the dressing over the salad and toss until well combined.

Serve immediately.

31. Beetroot Dip with Feta and Mint

Ingredients:

1 large beet, roasted and peeled
2 oz feta cheese, crumbled
1/4 cup Greek yogurt
2 tbsp fresh mint, chopped
1 clove garlic, minced
2 tbsp olive oil
Salt and pepper, to taste

Instructions:

In a food processor, pulse the roasted beet until it's finely chopped.

Add the crumbled feta cheese, Greek yogurt, chopped fresh mint, and minced garlic.

Pulse until everything is combined.

While the food processor is running, slowly drizzle in the olive oil.

Season with salt and pepper, to taste.

Serve with crackers or pita bread for dipping.

32. Beetroot and Chickpea Patties

Ingredients:

1 large beet, roasted and grated
1 can chickpeas, drained and rinsed
1/2 onion, finely chopped
1/4 cup flour
1/4 cup breadcrumbs
1 egg, beaten
2 tbsp olive oil
Salt and pepper, to taste
Instructions:

In a mixing bowl, combine the grated beet, chickpeas, finely chopped onion, flour, breadcrumbs, and beaten egg.
2. Season with salt and pepper, to taste.

Mix everything together until well combined.
Form the mixture into small patties.
Heat olive oil in a large skillet over medium heat.
Add the patties to the hot skillet and fry until golden brown on both sides, about 2-3 minutes per side.
Drain on a paper towel and serve warm.

MAIN COURSE

33. Spanish mackerel grilled with apples and beets

Makes: 4 Servings

INGREDIENTS

- 2 Spanish mackerel (about 2 pounds each), scaled and cleaned, with gills removed
- 2¼ cups Fennel Brine
- 1 tablespoon olive oil
- 1 medium onion, finely chopped
- 2 medium beets, roasted, boiled, grilled, or canned; finely chopped
- 1 tart apple, peeled, cored, and finely chopped
- 1 garlic clove, minced
- 1 tablespoon finely chopped fresh dill or fennel fronds
- 2 tablespoons fresh goat cheese
- 1 lime, cut into 8 wedges

INSTRUCTIONS:

a) Rinse the fish and put it in a 1-gallon zipper-lock bag with the brine, press out the air, and seal the bag. Refrigerate for 2 to 6 hours.

b) Heat the oil in a large skillet over medium heat. Add the onions and sauté until tender, about 3 minutes. Add the beets and apple and sauté until the apple is tender, about 4 minutes. Stir in the garlic and dill and heat through, about 1 minute. Cool the mixture to room temperature and stir in the goat cheese.

c) Meanwhile light a grill for direct medium heat, about 375¡F.

d) Remove the fish from the brine and pat dry. Discard the brine. Stuff the cavities of the fish with the cooled beet and apple mixture and secure with string, if needed.

e) Brush the grill grate and coat it with oil. Grill the fish until the skin is crisp and the fish looks opaque on the surface but is still filmy and moist in the middle (130¼F on an instant-read thermometer), 5 to 7 minutes per side. Remove the fish to a serving platter and serve with the lime wedges.

34. Beetroot risotto

Makes: 4

INGREDIENTS:
- 50g butter
- 1 onion, finely chopped
- 250g risotto rice
- 150ml white wine
- 1 liter vegetable stock
- 300g cooked beetroot
- 1 lemon, zested and juiced
- flat-leaf parsley a small bunch, roughly chopped
- 125g soft goat's cheese
- a handful of walnuts, toasted and chopped

INSTRUCTIONS:
a) Melt the butter in a deep frying pan and cook the onion with some seasoning for 10 minutes until soft. Tip in the rice and stir until every grain is coated, then pour in the wine and bubble for 5 minutes.

b) Add the stock a ladle at a time, while stirring, only adding more once the previous batch has been absorbed.

c) Meanwhile, take ½ the beetroot and whizz it in a small blender until smooth, and chop the remainder.

d) Once the rice is cooked, stir through the whizzed and chopped beetroots, lemon zest and juice, and most of the parsley. Divide between plates and top with a crumbling of goat's cheese, the walnuts, and the remaining parsley.

35. Beet Sliders with Microgreens

Makes: 4 Servings

INGREDIENTS:

BEETS

- 1 clove garlic, slightly smashed and peeled
- 2 carrots peeled, trimmed
- Pinch Salt and pepper
- 1 onion, peeled and quartered
- 4 beets
- 1 tablespoon caraway seeds
- 2 stalks of celery rinsed, trimmed

DRESSING:

- ½ cup mayonnaise
- ⅓ cup buttermilk
- ½ cup chopped parsley, chives, tarragon, or thyme
- 1 tablespoon lemon juice fresh squeezed
- 1 teaspoon anchovy paste
- 1 clove garlic chopped
- Salt & pepper

TOPPING:

- Slider buns
- 1 thinly sliced red onion
- Handful Mixed microgreens

INSTRUCTIONS:

DRESSING

a) Combine buttermilk, herbs, mayonnaise, lemon juice, anchovy paste, garlic, salt, and pepper.

BEETS

b) In a Dutch oven, boil beets, celery, carrots, onions, garlic, caraway seeds, salt, and pepper for 55 minutes.

c) Peel the beets and slice them into slices.

d) Sauté beet slices for 3 minutes on each side in a cooking spray-coated pan.

TO ASSEMBLE

e) Arrange the slider buns on a plate, and top them with beet, vinaigrette, red onions, and micro greens.

f) Enjoy.

Shrimp with Amaranth & Goat Cheese

Makes: 4

INGREDIENTS:
- 2 Beets Spiralized
- 4 oz Goat Cheese Softened
- ½ cup Arugula Microgreens Lightly chopped
- ½ cup Amaranth Microgreens Lightly chopped
- 1 pound Shrimp
- 1 cup Chopped Walnuts
- ¼ cup Raw Cane Sugar
- 1 tablespoons Butter
- 2 tablespoons Extra Virgin Olive Oil

INSTRUCTIONS:
a) Set out goat cheese to soften for 30 minutes before you start preparations.

b) Preheat oven to 375 degrees

c) Heat a skillet over moderate heat.

d) Add walnuts, sugar, and butter to the skillet and stir frequently over moderate heat.

e) Stir constantly once the sugar begins to melt.

f) Once walnuts are coated immediately transfer them to a sheet of parchment paper and separate the nuts so they don't harden stuck together. Set aside

g) Cut beets into spirals.

h) Toss spirals with olive oil and sea salt.

i) Spread out beets on a cookie sheet and bake in the oven for 20 - 25 minutes.

j) Rinse shrimp and add to a saucepan.

k) Fill a pan with water and sea salt. Bring to a boil.

l) Drain water and put it in an ice bath to stop cooking.

m) Clip and lightly chop arugula microgreens. Set aside.

n) Add microgreens to softened cheese, leaving aside a few pinches of each microgreen.

o) Blend microgreens and cheese.

p) Scrape the cheese mixture into a ball.

q) Plate beets.

r) Add a spoonful of cheese on top of the beets.

s) Place walnuts around the plate.

t) Add shrimp and sprinkle with remaining microgreens, salt, and cracked pepper.

Makes: 4 servings

INGREDIENTS:
- 1¼ cup Fresh beet juice
- Fruity olive oil
- 1 teaspoon White wine vinegar
- Kosher Salt; to taste
- Freshly ground black pepper; to taste
- 1¼ pounds Fresh sea scallops
- A few drops of Fresh lemon juice
- 1 pound Young kale leaves; tough center core removed
- A few drops of Sherry vinegar
- Fresh chives; cut into sticks
- Tiny dice of yellow bell pepper

INSTRUCTIONS:
a) Place beet juice in a non-reactive saucepan and boil until reduced to approximately ½ cup.

b) Off heat, whisk 2 to 3 tablespoons of olive oil slowly into a reduction to thicken the sauce. Whisk in white wine vinegar, salt, and pepper to taste. Set aside and keep warm.

c) Lightly oil the scallops and season with salt, pepper, and a few drops of lemon juice.

d) Brush kale leaves with oil and season lightly. Grill kale on both sides until the leaves are slightly charred and cooked through.

e) Grill scallops until just cooked (center should be slightly opaque). Arrange kale attractively in the center of warm plates and drizzle a few drops of sherry vinegar over it.

f) Place scallops on top and spoon beet sauce around. Garnish with chive sticks and yellow pepper and serve immediately.

37. Beet & Barley Risotto

Makes: 6

INGREDIENTS
- 2 red or yellow beets (about 1½ pounds total), or 1½ pounds baby beets, stems and leaves reserved
- Extra virgin olive oil
- Kosher salt
- 10 cups chicken stock
- 2 tablespoons unsalted butter
- 1 cup minced yellow onion (about 1 medium onion)
- 2 cloves garlic, minced
- 2 cups pearled barley
- ½ cup dry white wine (such as sauvignon blanc or pinot grigio)
- ¼ cup crème fraîche
- 2 teaspoons red wine vinegar
- Freshly ground black pepper
- ¼ pound ricotta salata cheese, grated

INSTRUCTIONS
a) Prepare the beets. Preheat the oven to 425°F. Rinse the stems and greens (leaves) thoroughly. Thinly slice the stems and coarsely chop the leaves, keeping them separate. Trim off the stem ends of the bulbs; thoroughly scrub the bulbs under cold water.

b) Roast and grate the beets. Arrange the beet bulbs in a small baking dish. Add enough water to come halfway up the sides of the beets. Drizzle with olive oil and season generously with salt. Cover the baking dish with aluminum foil and tightly seal. Roast for 1 hour, or until tender when pierced with a fork. When cool enough to handle, but still warm, use a paper towel and your fingers to gently rub the skin off the beets; discard the skins. Use a box grater to coarsely grate the beets. Set aside.

c) Cook the beet greens. While the beets are roasting, heat a pot of salted water to boiling on high. Add the chopped beet greens (leaves) and cook for 4 to 6 minutes, until softened. Transfer to a fine-mesh strainer to drain; use a spoon to press down on the greens to release as much liquid as possible. Set aside.

d) Warm the stock and sweat the aromatics. In a saucepan, heat the chicken stock to simmering on medium. Turn off the heat. In a large, high-sided saucepan, heat 2 tablespoons olive oil and 1 tablespoon of the butter on medium-low until the butter is melted. Add the onion, garlic, and beet stems and season with salt. Cook, stirring occasionally, for 3 to 5 minutes, until softened and fragrant but not browned.

e) Toast the barley. Add the barley. Cook, stirring occasionally, for 4 to 6 minutes, until the barley starts to puff slightly. Add the wine and cook, stirring frequently, for 30 seconds to 1 minute, until absorbed. Season with salt and stir to combine.

f) Add the stock. Add 2 cups of the stock and cook, stirring frequently, for 8 to 10 minutes, until most of the liquid has been absorbed. Repeat with the remaining 8 cups stock, adding the stock 2 cups at a time and stirring until most of the liquid is absorbed before each addition, for 22 to 28 minutes total.

g) Finish the risotto. Add the grated beets and cook, stirring frequently, for 2 to 3 minutes, until well combined. Add the beet greens and season with salt. Cook, stirring frequently, for 30 seconds to 1 minute, until warmed through. Add the crème fraîche, the remaining 1 tablespoon butter, and the vinegar. Cook, stirring constantly, for 2 to 3 minutes, until thoroughly combined and thickened. Remove from the heat. Season with salt and pepper. Transfer to a serving dish, top with the cheese, and serve.

38. Beetroot and Feta Stuffed Chicken

Ingredients:

4 boneless, skinless chicken breasts
1 large beet, roasted and grated
4 oz feta cheese, crumbled
1/4 cup chopped fresh parsley
2 cloves garlic, minced
2 tbsp olive oil
Salt and pepper, to taste

Instructions:

Preheat the oven to 375°F (190°C).

In a mixing bowl, combine the grated beet, crumbled feta cheese, chopped fresh parsley, minced garlic, olive oil, salt, and pepper.

Slice a pocket in the side of each chicken breast.

Stuff each chicken breast with the beet and feta mixture.

Secure the pockets with toothpicks.

Heat a large skillet over medium-high heat.

Add the stuffed chicken breasts to the skillet and cook for 3-4 minutes per side, until golden brown.

Transfer the chicken breasts to a baking dish.

Bake for 20-25 minutes or until the chicken is cooked through.

Serve hot.

Ingredients:

1 large beet, roasted and diced
8 oz mushrooms, sliced
1 onion, finely chopped
2 cloves garlic, minced
1 cup Arborio rice
1/2 cup white wine
3 cups vegetable stock
1/4 cup grated Parmesan cheese
2 tbsp butter
2 tbsp olive oil
Salt and pepper, to taste
Instructions:

In a large pot, heat the olive oil over medium heat.

Add the finely chopped onion and minced garlic and sauté until soft and translucent.

Add the sliced mushrooms and roasted diced beet and stir until combined.

Add the Arborio rice and stir until the rice is coated in oil.

Add the white wine and stir until the wine is absorbed.

Gradually add the vegetable stock, one ladle at a time, stirring continuously until each ladle of stock is absorbed before adding the next one.

Continue cooking the risotto until the rice is tender and creamy.

Remove from the heat and stir in the grated Parmesan cheese and butter.

Season with salt and pepper, to taste.

Serve immediately.

40. Beet and Goat Cheese Risotto

Ingredients:

2 large beets, roasted and grated
1 onion, diced
2 cloves garlic, minced
1 cup Arborio rice
1/2 cup white wine
4 cups vegetable broth
4 oz goat cheese
2 tbsp olive oil
Salt and pepper, to taste
Instructions:

In a large pot, heat the olive oil over medium heat.

Add the diced onion and minced garlic and sauté until soft and translucent.

Add the Arborio rice and stir until coated in oil.

Add the white wine and stir until combined.

Add the vegetable broth, one cup at a time, stirring constantly and allowing the broth to be absorbed before adding the next cup.

When the rice is cooked, add the grated roasted beets and stir until combined.

Add the goat cheese and stir until melted.

Season with salt and pepper, to taste.

Serve immediately.

41. Beet and Mushroom Stir-Fry

Ingredients:

2 large beets, peeled and julienned
1 cup sliced mushrooms
1 onion, sliced
2 cloves garlic, minced
1 tbsp grated ginger
2 tbsp soy sauce
2 tbsp sesame oil
2 tbsp olive oil
Salt and pepper, to taste
Instructions:

In a large wok or frying pan, heat the olive oil and sesame oil over high heat.

Add the julienned beets and stir-fry for 2-3 minutes.

Add the sliced mushrooms, sliced onion, minced garlic, and grated ginger and stir-fry for an additional 2-3 minutes.

Add the soy sauce and stir-fry for another 1-2 minutes.

Season with salt and pepper, to taste.

Serve with rice or noodles.

SALADS

Makes: 12 Servings

INGREDIENTS:
- 3 golden beets, trimmed
- 2 tablespoons lime juice
- 1 teaspoon orange zest
- 2 tablespoon sunflower seed
- 1 tablespoon minced Parsley
- 3 tablespoons goat cheese
- 1 tablespoon minced sage
- 2 tablespoons orange juice
- 1 garlic clove, minced

INSTRUCTIONS:
a) Preheat the air fryer to 400. Fold heavy-duty foil around the beets and place them on a tray in the air fryer basket.

b) Cook until tender, 50 minutes. Peel, halve and slice beets; place in a bowl.

c) Add lime juice, orange juice, and salt.

d) Sprinkle with parsley, sage, garlic, and orange zest, and top with goat cheese and sunflower kernels.

Makes: 4 servings

INGREDIENTS:
- 1 medium bunch of beets with greens
- 1⁄3 cup fresh lemon juice
- 2 tablespoons light brown sugar
- ½ cup dried apricots
- Salt and freshly ground black pepper

INSTRUCTIONS:

a) Preheat the oven to 400°F. Remove the greens from the beets and wash them well, then cut them crosswise into ½-inch-wide strips. Set aside. Scrub the beets well.

b) Wrap the beets tightly in aluminum foil and bake until tender, about 1 hour.

c) While the beets are roasting, place the apricots in a small heatproof bowl and cover them with boiling water to soften for about 10 minutes. Drain and cut into thin slivers and set aside.

d) When the beets are roasted, unwrap them and set them aside to cool. When cool enough to handle, peel the beets and cut them into 1⁄4-inch-thick slices, and set aside.

e) In a small saucepan, combine the lemon juice, sugar, and sliced apricots and bring to a boil. Reduce heat to low and simmer for 5 minutes. Set aside.

f) Place the reserved greens in a skillet with 2 tablespoons of water. Cover and bring to a boil, then reduce the heat to medium and cook until the greens are wilted and the liquid is evaporated about 2 minutes. Stir the apricot-lemon mixture into the greens and season with salt and pepper to taste. Add the beet slices and cook until they are heated through about 3 minutes. Serve immediately.

44. Beet Fennel Salad

Makes: 2 Servings

INGREDIENTS:
- 3 cups chopped greens
- ¼ bulb of fennel, sliced thin
- ½ cup chopped cooked broccoli florets
- ½ cup chopped beets
- 1 to 2 tablespoons extra virgin olive oil
- Juice of ½ lemon

INSTRUCTIONS:
a) In a large bowl, mix the greens, fennel, broccoli, and beets.
b) Toss with olive oil and lemon juice.

45. Beet Hazelnut Salad

Makes: 2 Servings

INGREDIENTS:
- 2 cups baby spinach
- ½ avocado, diced
- 1 cup beets, diced
- ¼ cup hazelnuts
- 2 tablespoons extra virgin olive oil
- 1 tablespoon balsamic vinegar

INSTRUCTIONS:

a)   Put spinach, avocado, beets, and hazelnuts in a bowl. Dress with oil and vinegar.

b)   Toss and enjoy.

46. Beetroot and Tomato Salad

Makes: 2 Servings

INGREDIENTS:

- ½ cup fresh tomatoes – chopped
- ½ cup cooked beetroot – chopped
- 1 Tablespoon vegetable oil
- ¼ Tablespoons mustard seeds
- ¼ Tablespoons of cumin seeds
- Pinch turmeric
- 2 pinches asafoetida
- 4 curry leaves
- Salt to taste
- Sugar to taste
- 2 Tablespoons peanut powder
- Freshly chopped coriander leaves

INSTRUCTIONS:

a) Heat the oil before adding the mustard seeds.

b) When they start to pop, add the cumin, turmeric, curry leaves, and asafoetida.

c) Toss beetroot and tomato with spice mixture, peanut powder, salt, sugar, and coriander leaves to taste.

47. Mixed Green Salad with Beets

Makes: 4 servings

INGREDIENTS:
- 2 medium beets, tops trimmed
- 2 tablespoons calcium-fortified orange juice
- 1 ½ teaspoon honey
- ⅛ teaspoon salt
- ⅛ teaspoon black pepper
- ¼ cup olive oil
- 2 tablespoons raw, hulled sunflower seeds
- 1 orange, cut into segments
- 3 cups packed mixed salad greens
- ¼cup reduced fat feta cheese, crumbled

INSTRUCTIONS:

a) In a medium saucepan, cover the beets with water. Bring to a boil, then lower to low heat.

b) Cook for 20-30 minutes, or until fork tender, covered. Beets should be drained.

c) When the beets are cool enough to handle, peel them under running water and cut them into wedges.

d) In the meantime, stir together the orange juice, honey, garlic, salt, and pepper in a jar.

e) Shake in the olive oil until the dressing is smooth. Remove from the equation.

f) In a small sauté pan, melt the butter over medium-low heat.

g) In a dry sauté pan, toast sunflower seeds for 2-3 minutes, or until aromatic.

h) Toss beets, sunflower seeds, orange segments, mixed greens, and feta cheese in a large serving bowl.

i) Serve with a drizzle of dressing.

48. Rainbow Beet and Pistachio Salad

Makes: 2 Servings

INGREDIENTS:
- 2 small bunches of rainbow beets, trimmed
- Canola oil for beets

BASIL LEMON OLIVE OIL:
- 2 cups loosely packed basil
- scant ¼ cup olive oil
- ½ juice of a lemon
- pinch of kosher salt
- 1 Tablespoon chopped Pistachios
- 1 cup of Micro Greens
- Citrus Herb Salt – optional

INSTRUCTIONS:
a) Toss the beets with 1–2 tablespoons of canola oil until they are gently coated.

b) Place beets on a rimmed baking sheet, cover with foil, and roast on the grill for 30-45 minutes, or until tender and browned.

c) Remove the peels from the beets and discard them.

d) To make the basil olive oil, blend all of the ingredients in a blender until smooth.

e) Drizzle a small amount of basil olive oil on the bottom of two small plates.

f) On each plate, scatter a small number of microgreens, half of the beets, citrus herb salt, and pistachios.

g) Place the remaining micro greens on top of each plate.

49. Pink Salad

Makes: 2 Servings

INGREDIENTS

SALAD

- 4 whole carrots
- ⅓ medium red onion, slivered
- 1 large beet
- 1 pink grapefruit, sectioned
- 1 handful of roughly chopped pistachios

VINAIGRETTE

- ½ cup olive oil
- ¼ cup rice wine vinegar
- 1 teaspoon mustard
- 1 teaspoon maple syrup
- 1-2 cloves garlic, minced
- salt and pepper to taste

INSTRUCTIONS:

a) Slice your beets into medium wedges and place in a microwaveable container, cover, and micro until fork tender. Mine took 6 ½ minutes. I choose not to peel mine as I don't mind the skin but do what you like.

b) Using a carrot peeler shave off long strips from each carrot until you reach the core and can shave no more. Save the cores for munching on later.

c) In a large bowl place, all of your salad ingredients except the pistachios.

d) In another bowl place all of the dressing ingredients and whisk until emulsified.

e) When you are ready to serve the salad toss it with enough dressing to coat it and reserve the rest for tomorrow's salad.

f) Sprinkle on the pistachios and you are good to go.

50. Yellow Beet Salad With Pears

Makes: 2 Servings

INGREDIENTS:
- 3 to 4 medium yellow beets
- 2 tablespoons white balsamic vinegar
- 3 tablespoons vegan mayonnaise, homemade (see Vegan Mayonnaise) or store-bought
- 3 tablespoons vegan sour cream, homemade (see Tofu Sour Cream) or store-bought
- 1 tablespoon soy milk
- 1½ tablespoons minced fresh dillweed
- 1 tablespoon minced shallot
- ½ teaspoon salt
- ¼ teaspoon freshly ground black pepper
- 2 ripe Bosc pears
- Juice of 1 lemon
- 1 small head of red leaf lettuce, torn into bite-size pieces

INSTRUCTIONS:
a) Steam the beets until tender, then cool and peel them. Cut the beets into matchsticks and place them in a shallow bowl. Add the vinegar and toss to coat. Set aside.

b) In a small bowl, combine the mayonnaise, sour cream, soy milk, dillweed, shallot, salt, and pepper. Set aside.

c) Core the pears and cut them into 1/4-inch dice. Place the pears in a medium bowl, add the lemon juice, and toss gently to combine. Divide the lettuce among 4 salad plates and spoon the pears and the beets on top. Drizzle the dressing over the salad, sprinkle with pecans, and serve.

51. Beet and tofu salad

Makes: 4 Servings

INGREDIENTS:
- 3 Beets; peeled OR 5 small beets
- 1 small Red Bermuda onion; sliced into thin rings and separated
- 1 pounds Firm or extra-firm tofu; drained and cut into ½-inch cubes
- ¼ cup Red wine vinegar
- 2 tablespoons Balsamic vinegar
- ¼ Cup olive oil; or less to taste
- ½ teaspoon Dried oregano
- Salt and pepper

INSTRUCTIONS:
a) Cook beets until just tender when tested with a fork: large beets might take 45 minutes to boil and cook.

b) When cool enough to handle, slice beets in half, then slice each half into ¼-inch slices. Place in a bowl. Add the dressing. Toss gently to combine.

c) Taste for seasonings. Serve immediately or chilled. Toss again just before serving.

52. Grapefruit, beet, and blue cheese salad

Makes: 1 Serving

INGREDIENTS:

- ½ bunch Watercress; coarse stems discarded
- 1 Grapefruit
- 1 ounce Blue cheese; cut into small thin slices
- 2 Peeled cooked beets, grated coarse
- 4 teaspoons Extra-virgin olive oil
- 1 tablespoon Balsamic vinegar
- Coarse salt to taste
- Coarsely ground pepper to taste

INSTRUCTIONS:

a) Divide the watercress between 2 salad plates and arrange grapefruit sections and cheese decoratively on top.

b) In a small bowl toss together beets, 2 teaspoons oil, and vinegar and divide between salads.

c) Drizzle salads with remaining oil and season with salt and pepper.

53. Potato salad

Makes: 4 Servings

INGREDIENTS:
- 1 kg of blue potatoes
- 200 g beetroot
- Salt
- Pepper
- 2 bunch of spring onions
- 250 g sour cream
- 5 tablespoons white wine vinegar
- 2 bunch of radishes
- ¼ bed of cress
- ¼ Beet

INSTRUCTIONS:
a) Wash potatoes and beets thoroughly and cook in plenty of salted water for about 15 minutes.
b) Wash the spring onions, clean and cut into thin strips.
c) Lay the spring onions in ice water so that they roll up.
d) Mix sour cream and vinegar — season with salt and pepper.
e) Drain potatoes, put them off, peel and dice roughly.
f) Rinse beets with cold water, peel and cut into thin slices.
g) Thoroughly wash radishes, clean and quarter.
h) Mix potatoes, beetroot, spring onions and radishes with the dressing.
i) Arrange in bowls. Sprinkle with cress.

54. Saffron quinoa and roasted beet salad

Makes: 6 Servings

INGREDIENTS:
- 6 tablespoons Extra-virgin olive oil
- 2 tablespoons Fresh lemon juice
- 2 smalls Clove garlic; minced
- ½ teaspoon Coarse salt
- ½ teaspoon Ground cumin
- ¼ teaspoon Red pepper flakes; up to ½
- 4 smalls Beets with greens attached; up to 5
- 1 cup Uncooked quinoa
- 2 cups Vegetable broth
- ⅛ teaspoon Saffron threads
- 5 teaspoons Olive oil
- 2 ounces Thinly sliced shallots; (½ cup)
- 3 mediums Clove garlic; minced
- 1½ tablespoons Fresh lemon juice
- ¼ teaspoon Salt

INSTRUCTIONS:
a) Preheat oven to 400F.
b) In a small bowl, whisk together all ingredients.
c) Adjust seasoning to taste and set aside.
d) Wash beets and trim off greens, leaving about 1 inch attached. Reserve beet greens. Wrap each beet individually in foil and bake until tender when pierced with a thin knife, 45 minutes to 1 hour. Set aside to cool.
e) When beets are cool enough to handle, peel and thinly slice. Place beets in a small bowl, add 2 to 3 tablespoons of the marinade, and toss gently.
f) Place quinoa in a fine-meshed sieve and rinse under cold water until foam subsides. Transfer quinoa to a small saucepan, add broth and saffron and bring to a boil. Reduce heat to low, cover, and simmer until broth is absorbed 13 to 15 minutes.

g) Meanwhile, in a medium skillet, heat 3 teaspoons of olive oil over medium-high heat. Add shallots and cook until crisp, stirring often for about 3 minutes.

h) Drain on paper towels and set aside.

i) Transfer the cooked quinoa mixture to a medium bowl and toss with 3 to 4 more tablespoons of marinade. (Remaining marinade can be covered and refrigerated for up to 3 days.) Remove and discard thick stems from beet greens; coarsely chop leaves. In a large skillet, heat the remaining 2 teaspoons of oil over medium heat. Add garlic and cook, stirring often, for 1 minute. Add beet greens and cook until wilted, 1 to 2 minutes. Stir in lemon juice and salt. Season with pepper.

j) To serve, divide sliced beets among serving plates and arrange them around the rim. Mound ¼ cup of quinoa mixture in the center of the beets. Top with beet greens, garnish with fried shallots and serve.

Makes: 4

INGREDIENTS
2 pounds baby beets (red, yellow, and/or Chioggia), trimmed, stems and leaves reserved
Extra virgin olive oil
Kosher salt
½ cup minced shallots (about 2 medium shallots)
7 tablespoons red wine vinegar
Freshly ground black pepper
8 ounces fresh soft goat cheese
3 tablespoons thinly sliced fresh chives
½ cup all-purpose flour
2 large eggs
1 cup panko breadcrumbs
Grapeseed oil or other vegetable oil
1 cup fresh flat-leaf parsley, coarsely chopped
½ cup toasted walnuts, coarsely chopped

1. Roast the beets. Preheat the oven to 450°F. Arrange the beets in a single layer in a 9 by 13-inch baking dish. Add enough water to come halfway up the sides of the beets. Drizzle with olive oil and season generously with salt. Cover the baking dish with aluminum foil and tightly seal. Roast the beets for 1 hour to 1 hour 15 minutes, or until tender when pierced with a fork.
2. Make the marinade. While the beets roast, in a medium bowl, combine ¼ cup shallots, 6 tablespoons of the red wine vinegar, and ½ teaspoon salt.
3. Peel and marinate the beets. When the beets are cool enough to handle, but still warm, use a paper towel to gently rub their skin off. Halve or quarter the beets and transfer them to a large bowl. Season with salt and pepper to taste. Pour the marinade over the beets; toss to coat. Let stand for 30 minutes to marinate.
4. Cook the beet stems and leaves. Cut the beet stems into 2-inch pieces. Roll the leaves into a tight log and cut at an angle into long,

1-inch-wide strips. In a sauté pan, heat 1 tablespoon olive oil on medium until hot. Add the stems and season with salt. Cook, stirring occasionally, for 3 to 5 minutes, until slightly tender. Add the beet leaves and season with salt and pepper. Cook, stirring occasionally, for 2 to 4 minutes, until wilted. Stir in the remaining 1 tablespoon red wine vinegar. Remove from the heat.

5. Form the goat cheese rounds. Remove the goat cheese from the refrigerator and let stand at room temperature for about 10 minutes, until slightly softened. In a bowl, combine the chives, the remaining ¼ cup shallots, and the goat cheese. Season with 1 teaspoon salt and ½ teaspoon pepper. Mix until thoroughly combined. Use your hands to form into four equal balls, then carefully flatten each into a ¼-inch-thick round. Transfer the rounds to a plate.

6. Bread the goat cheese. Spread the flour on a shallow dish and season with salt and pepper. Crack the eggs into a shallow bowl and beat until just combined. Spread the breadcrumbs on another shallow dish. Working with one at a time, thoroughly coat the goat cheese rounds in the flour; tap off any excess. Dip both sides in the eggs, letting the excess drip off, then in the breadcrumbs; press to make sure the breadcrumbs adhere. Transfer the rounds to a plate and cover with plastic wrap; chill in the refrigerator until just before frying.

7. Crisp the goat cheese. Just before serving, remove the goat cheese rounds from the refrigerator. Line a plate with paper towels. In a cast-iron skillet or sauté pan, heat a thin layer of grapeseed oil on medium-high until hot. The oil is hot enough when a few breadcrumbs sizzle immediately when added to the pan. Add the goat cheese rounds. Cook for 2 to 4 minutes per side, until golden brown and crispy. Transfer to the plate and season with salt and pepper.

8. Finish and serve the salad. Add the parsley and walnuts to the roasted beets; stir to thoroughly combine. Divide the beet greens (leaves), stems, and roasted beets among serving dishes. Top each with a goat cheese round and serve.

56. Cumin Roasted Root Vegetables

Makes: 2

INGREDIENTS:
- 2 red beets
- 1/4 cup peanuts
- 1 teaspoon ground cumin
- 3 carrots
- 1/2 cup white quinoa
- 3 parsnips
- 2 tablespoons white sesame seeds
- 1 lime
- 1/2 teaspoon smoked paprika
- 1 shallot
- 1 avocado
- 1 jalapeño
- 4 tablespoons vegetable broth, divided
- Salt and pepper to taste

INSTRUCTIONS:
a) Preheat the oven to 425 °F.
b) Peel and cut the carrots and parsnips into 1-inch pieces. Coarsely chop the peanuts.
c) The lime should be zested, halved, and juiced.
d) Peel and dice 2 tablespoons of shallot.
e) Mince 2 tablespoons of Jalapeño.
f) Peel the beets and cut them into ½-inch thick wedges.
g) Add cumin, sliced carrots, sliced parsnips, 1 tablespoon of vegetable broth, and a pinch of salt to one side of a baking sheet and toss.
h) Add wedged beets, 1 tablespoon vegetable broth, and a pinch of salt to the other side of the baking sheet and toss.
i) Roast the root vegetables for 25 to 28 minutes or until tender.
j) Combine the quinoa, 1 cup of water, and a pinch of salt in a medium saucepan over high heat.

k) Boil and cook for at least 12 to 15 minutes, or until the spirals burst, and the water is absorbed.

l) In a small bowl, combine the lime zest, half of the lime juice, diced shallot, and minced jalapeño.

m)   In a small skillet, toast the chopped peanuts and sesame seeds over medium heat until golden brown for 2 to 3 minutes.

n) Toss the toasted peanuts and sesame seeds with the shallot and jalapeño in a small bowl.

o) Add 1 tablespoon of vegetable broth, 1 teaspoon paprika, and a pinch of salt.

p) Combine the sesame peanut salsa with a fork. Cut the Avocado in half.

q) Scoop the avocado flesh into a small bowl and season with salt and the remaining lime juice to taste. Using a fork, mash until smooth.

r) Divide the quinoa among the plates.

s) Serve with smashed avocado on each plate.

t) Serve with cumin-roasted vegetables and a drizzle of peanut sesame salsa on top.

57. Kale Lentil & Roasted Beet Salad

Makes: 3

INGREDIENTS:

- 1 medium beet, rinsed, cleaned, dried, quartered
- 1/2 cup green lentils, rinsed, cleaned
- 3 medium leeks, trimmed, sliced, chopped
- 1 cup vegetable stock
- 4 big handfuls kale, baby spinach
- 1/4 teaspoon each salt and pepper
- 2 tablespoons vegetable broth
- Tahini Dressing
- 1/4 cup tahini
- 4 tablespoons vegetable broth
- 1/2 medium lemon, juiced
- 2 tablespoons maple syrup
- 1 pinch each salt and pepper

INSTRUCTIONS:

a) Start preheating the oven to 400 °F and brush the baking sheet lightly using the vegetable broth.

b) Add lentils and vegetable stock (or water) to a small saucepan and bring a rapid simmer over medium-high heat.

c) Reduce heat and simmer for 20-30 minutes until all liquid is absorbed. Set aside.

d) Add chopped leeks and beets to the baking sheet, drizzle with vegetable broth, and season with salt and pepper. Toss to coat.

e) Bake for at least 15-20 minutes until fragrant and lightly browned, then set aside.

f) While vegetables and lentils are cooking, prepare the dressing by adding all ingredients to a mixing bowl, then whisk to combine. Taste and adjust seasonings.

g) Add the kale to a separate mixing bowl with a sprinkle of vegetable broth and lemon juice and massage with hands to soften. For the greens, skip this step.

h) Add beets, greens, leeks, and lentils to a large mixing bowl, add dressing and toss to coat. Serve and enjoy!

Makes: 4 TO 6

INGREDIENTS:

- 2 pounds beets, trimmed, peeled, and cut into ¾-inch pieces
- 1⅛ teaspoons table salt, divided
- 1¼ cups plain Greek yogurt
- ¼ cup minced fresh cilantro, divided
- 3 tablespoons extra-virgin olive oil, divided
- 2 teaspoons grated fresh ginger
- 1 teaspoon grated lime zest plus 2 tablespoons juice, divided
- 1 garlic clove, minced
- ½ teaspoon ground cumin
- ½ teaspoon ground coriander
- ¼ teaspoon pepper
- 5 ounces (5 cups) watercress, torn into bite-size pieces
- ¼ cup shelled pistachios, toasted and chopped, divided

INSTRUCTIONS:

a) Combine beets, ⅓ cup water, and ½ teaspoon salt in large bowl. Cover and microwave until beets can be easily pierced with paring knife, 25 to 30 minutes, stirring halfway through microwaving. Drain beets in colander and let cool.

b) Whisk yogurt, 3 tablespoons cilantro, 2 tablespoons oil, ginger, lime zest and 1 tablespoon juice, garlic, cumin, coriander, pepper, and ½ teaspoon salt together in bowl. Slowly stir in up to 3 tablespoons water until mixture has consistency of regular yogurt. Season with salt and pepper to taste. Spread yogurt mixture over serving platter.

c) Toss watercress with 2 tablespoons pistachios, 2 teaspoons oil, 1 teaspoon lime juice, and pinch salt in large bowl. Arrange watercress mixture over top of yogurt mixture, leaving 1-inch border of yogurt mixture. Toss beets with remaining 1 teaspoon oil, remaining 2 teaspoons lime juice, and remaining pinch salt in now-empty bowl.

d) Arrange beet mixture over top of watercress mixture. Sprinkle salad with remaining 1 tablespoon cilantro and remaining 2 tablespoons pistachios and serve.

59. Beetroot and Goat Cheese Salad

Ingredients:

4 large beets, roasted and sliced
4 oz goat cheese, crumbled
1/4 cup chopped walnuts
1/4 cup chopped fresh parsley
2 tbsp balsamic vinegar
2 tbsp olive oil
Salt and pepper, to taste
Instructions:

In a large mixing bowl, combine the roasted and sliced beets, crumbled goat cheese, chopped walnuts, and chopped fresh parsley.
In a separate small mixing bowl, whisk together the balsamic vinegar and olive oil.
Drizzle the dressing on top of the salad.
Season with salt and pepper, to taste.
Toss gently to combine.
Serve at room temperature.

60. Beet and Goat Cheese Salad

Ingredients:
2 large beets, roasted and sliced
2 cups mixed greens
2 oz goat cheese
1/4 cup chopped pecans
2 tbsp balsamic vinegar
2 tbsp olive oil
Salt and pepper, to taste

Instructions:
In a mixing bowl, combine the roasted and sliced beets, mixed greens, crumbled goat cheese, and chopped pecans.
In a separate small mixing bowl, whisk together the balsamic vinegar, olive oil, salt, and pepper.
Pour the dressing over the salad and toss until well combined.
Serve immediately.

61. Beet and Orange Salad

Ingredients:

4 medium beets, roasted and sliced
2 oranges, peeled and sliced
1/4 cup crumbled goat cheese
1/4 cup chopped walnuts
1/4 cup chopped fresh parsley
2 tbsp olive oil
2 tbsp balsamic vinegar
Salt and pepper, to taste
Instructions:

In a large mixing bowl, combine the sliced roasted beets, sliced oranges, crumbled goat cheese, chopped walnuts, and chopped fresh parsley.

In a separate small mixing bowl, whisk together the olive oil and balsamic vinegar.

Drizzle the dressing over the beet and orange mixture and toss to combine.

Season with salt and pepper, to taste.

Serve chilled or at room temperature.

SOUP

62. Beet Borscht

Makes: 2 Servings

INGREDIENTS:

- 1 can whole beets
- 4 cup water
- 1 whole onion, peeled
- salt
- 2 heaping Tablespoons sugar
- ¼-½ teaspoon sour salt

INSTRUCTIONS:

a) Simmer onion in water for 10 minutes. Add grated (shredded) beets with juice and all other ingredients.

b) Simmer for 5 minutes. more.

c) Taste and adjust seasonings.

d) Serve hot or cold.

63. Cabbage & beet soup

Makes: 8 Servings

INGREDIENTS:

- 1 Med Cabbage; sliced or wedge
- 3 Garlic; cloves minced
- Beet; bunch
- 3 Carrot; few
- 1 Lg Onion
- 2 Celery; stalks cut in 3rds
- 3 pounds Bone; meat/marrow bones
- 2 Lemon
- 2 cans Tomatoes; do not drain

INSTRUCTIONS:

a) Put meat and bones in an 8 or 12-qt stock pot. Put in cans of tomatoes, cover with water and bring to a boil.

b) In the meantime, get your veggies ready. Slice beets and carrots, others go in whole. When stock boils, skim off the top.

c) Put in beets, carrots, garlic, and other veggies. Turn the heat down to a simmer and keep the lid on askew.

d) After about an hour, put in garlic and sugar.

Makes: 6 Servings

INGREDIENTS:
- 5 Beets
- 3 cups Buttermilk
- ¾ cup Chopped green onions
- ⅔ cup Light sour cream
- 2 tablespoons Chopped fresh dill or coriander
- 1½ teaspoon Granulated sugar
- 1½ teaspoon White vinegar
- ¼ teaspoon Salt
- 1 cup Cucumber; (diced unpeeled)
- Fresh dill or coriander sprigs

INSTRUCTIONS:
a) In a saucepan of boiling salted water, cover and cook beets until tender and skins slip off easily about 25 minutes. Drain and let cool; slip off skins and cut into ¼-inch (5 mm) dice. Cover and refrigerate until chilled.

b) In a large bowl, whisk together buttermilk, ½ cup (125 mL) of onions, sour cream, dill, sugar, vinegar, and salt. Cover and refrigerate until chilled or for up to 6 hours. Taste and adjust seasoning.

c) Ladle buttermilk mixture into serving bowls. Swirl in beets and cucumber.

d) Garnish with remaining green onions and dill or coriander sprigs.

Makes: 4 servings

INGREDIENTS:
- 3 tablespoons Ghee
- 1 pinch of Cumin seeds
- 1 each Bay leaf
- 2½ tablespoons Sliced onion
- ¼ teaspoon Cayenne
- ¼ teaspoon Garam masala
- 1 medium Potato, diced
- ½ cup Green peas
- 15 ounces of Beets, cooked & diced
- ½ teaspoon Salt

INSTRUCTIONS:
a) Heat ghee & fry cumin seeds, bay leaf, spiced onion, cayenne & garam masala for 1 minute.

b) Add potato, peas & beets & cook gently for 2 minutes. Add salt & a little water.

c) Cook gently until the potato is tender.

d) Serve over rice.

66. Cream of beet soup

Makes: 6 servings

INGREDIENTS:

- 1 pounds Beets, peeled and coarsely chopped (about 3 medium)
- 1 large Onion, coarsely chopped
- 1 Fresh marjoram sprig OR
- 1 teaspoon Dried chopped fresh thyme
- 3 tablespoons Unsalted butter
- 1 quart Chicken or vegetable broth
- ½ cup Heavy cream
- 2 tablespoons Good red wine vinegar
- Salt
- Pepper
- ½ cup Heavy cream, lightly whipped
- Small croutons
- ¼ cup Chopped fresh herbs, such as dill or marjoram

INSTRUCTIONS:

a) Cook beets, onion, and marjoram in butter in a 4-quart pot over medium heat until onion begins to soften slightly, about 10 minutes. Add broth, partially cover the pot, and simmer for about 30 minutes, until the beets are completely soft.

b) Check them by trying to crush one against the side of the pot with a wooden spoon. Simmer longer if necessary.

c) Puree soup in a blender or food processor. If you want the soup to have a smoother texture, strain it through a medium-mesh strainer. Add cream or vinegar and bring the soup back to a simmer. Season with salt and pepper.

d) To serve, ladle into bowls and garnish with whipped cream, croutons, and herbs, or serve garnishes separately and let diners help themselves.

67. Spinach and beet soup

Makes: 8 Servings

INGREDIENTS:

- ½ cup Chickpeas
- 2 cups Spinach; chopped
- 1 cup Kidney beans
- 1 cup Fresh dill weed -or-
- ¼ cup Dried dill weed
- 1 cup Lentils
- 4 Beets; peeled & cubed small
- 1 large Onion; chopped (up to)
- 2 tablespoons Flour (up to)
- 2 Soup bones; optional
- Fried onions & dry mint leaves (for garnish)
- Salt & pepper to taste
- Oil for frying (up to)
- 8 cups Water

INSTRUCTIONS:

a) Soak the chickpeas & kidney beans for 2 hours or overnight. Cook the lentils in l-2 cups of water till soft but not mushy & set aside.

b) Brown the bones and onions in oil in a large kettle. Season to taste and add water, chickpeas, kidney beans, & beets. Cook until the chickpeas are soft.

c) Remove bones & add spinach, dill weed, and lentils. Stir occasionally. Meanwhile, brown flour in a little bit of oil and add to the soup to thicken it.

d) Put the soup on low heat & stir frequently until done. Serve in a bowl & garnish with fried onion or with dried mint leaves added to hot oil.

68. Beetroot Soup

Makes: 2 Servings

INGREDIENTS:
- 1 large beetroot
- 1 cup water
- 2 pinch cumin powder
- 2 pinch pepper
- 1 pinch cinnamon
- 4 pinch salt
- Squeeze of lemon
- ½ Tablespoon ghee

INSTRUCTIONS:
a) Boil the beetroot then peel.

b) Blend with the water and filter if desired.

c) Boil the mixture then add the remaining ingredients and serve.

69. Beet and Chickpea Curry

Ingredients:
2 large beets, peeled and diced
1 can chickpeas, drained and rinsed
1 onion, diced
2 cloves garlic, minced
1 tbsp grated ginger
1 tsp cumin
1 tsp coriander
1 tsp turmeric
1 tsp smoked paprika
1 can coconut milk
1/2 cup vegetable stock
2 tbsp olive oil
Salt and pepper, to taste

Instructions:
In a large pot, heat the olive oil over medium heat.

Add the diced onion, minced garlic, and grated ginger and sauté until soft and translucent.

Add the diced beets and stir until coated in oil.

Add the cumin, coriander, turmeric, and smoked paprika and stir until combined.

Add the chickpeas, coconut milk, and vegetable stock and stir until combined.

Bring the mixture to a simmer and cook until the beets are tender and the sauce has thickened, about 30-40 minutes.

Season with salt and pepper, to taste.

Serve with rice or naan bread.

70. Beetroot and Beef Stew

Ingredients:

2 lbs beef stew meat
2 large beets, peeled and diced
2 carrots, peeled and diced
1 onion, diced
2 cloves garlic, minced
1 cup beef broth
1 cup red wine
2 tbsp olive oil
2 tbsp flour
1 tbsp tomato paste
1 bay leaf
1 tsp dried thyme
Salt and pepper, to taste
Instructions:

In a large pot, heat the olive oil over medium-high heat.
Season the beef stew meat with salt and pepper and coat in flour.
Add the beef stew meat to the pot and brown on all sides.
Remove the beef stew meat from the pot and set aside.
Add the diced onion and minced garlic to the pot and sauté until soft and translucent.
Add the diced beets and diced carrots to the pot and stir until combined.
Add the tomato paste, bay leaf, and dried thyme and stir until combined.
Add the beef broth and red wine and stir until combined.
Return the beef stew meat to the pot and bring the mixture to a simmer.
Cover the pot with a lid and reduce the heat to low

71. Roasted Beet Soup

Ingredients:

4 medium beets, roasted
1 onion, chopped
2 cloves garlic, minced
4 cups vegetable broth
1/2 cup heavy cream
2 tbsp olive oil
Salt and pepper, to taste
Instructions:

Preheat oven to 400°F.

Wrap each beet individually in aluminum foil and roast for 45-60 minutes, or until tender.

Once the beets have cooled, peel them and chop into small pieces.

In a large pot, heat the olive oil over medium heat.

Add the chopped onion and minced garlic and sauté until soft and translucent.

Add the chopped roasted beets and vegetable broth to the pot and bring to a simmer.

Simmer for 10-15 minutes, or until the beets are very tender.

Puree the soup in a blender or with an immersion blender.

Stir in the heavy cream and season with salt and pepper to taste.

Serve hot.

72. Creamy Beet Soup

Ingredients:

4 medium beets, roasted and diced
1 onion, chopped
2 cloves garlic, minced
4 cups vegetable broth
1 cup heavy cream
2 tbsp olive oil
Salt and pepper, to taste
Instructions:

In a large pot, heat the olive oil over medium heat.

Add the chopped onion and minced garlic and sauté until soft and translucent.

Add the diced roasted beets and vegetable broth to the pot and bring to a simmer.

Simmer for 10-15 minutes, or until the beets are very tender.

Puree the soup in a blender or with an immersion blender.

Stir in the heavy cream and season with salt and pepper to taste.

Serve hot.

73. Spicy Beet Soup

Ingredients:

4 medium beets, peeled and diced
1 onion, chopped
2 cloves garlic, minced
4 cups vegetable broth
1 tsp ground cumin
1 tsp smoked paprika
1/2 tsp cayenne pepper
1/2 cup sour cream
2 tbsp olive oil
Salt and pepper, to taste

Instructions:
In a large pot, heat the olive oil over medium heat.
Add the chopped onion and minced garlic and sauté until soft and translucent.
Add the diced beets, vegetable broth, ground cumin, smoked paprika, and cayenne pepper to the pot and bring to a simmer.
4. Simmer for 30-45 minutes, or until the beets are very tender.

Puree the soup in a blender or with an immersion blender.

Stir in the sour cream and season with salt and pepper to taste.

Serve hot.

74. Beet and Carrot Soup

Ingredients:

2 medium beets, peeled and diced
2 medium carrots, peeled and diced
1 onion, chopped
2 cloves garlic, minced
4 cups vegetable broth
2 tbsp olive oil
Salt and pepper, to taste
Instructions:

In a large pot, heat the olive oil over medium heat.
Add the chopped onion and minced garlic and sauté until soft and translucent.
Add the diced beets, diced carrots, and vegetable broth to the pot and bring to a simmer.
Simmer for 30-45 minutes, or until the beets and carrots are very tender.
Puree the soup in a blender or with an immersion blender.
Season with salt and pepper to taste.
Serve hot.

SIDES

75. <u>Beets with Mustard Seeds and Coconut</u>

Makes: 3 Cups

INGREDIENTS:
- 1 tablespoon oil
- 1 teaspoon black mustard seeds
- 1 yellow or red onion, peeled and diced
- 2 teaspoons ground cumin
- 2 teaspoons ground coriander
- 1 teaspoon South Indian masala
- 1 tablespoon unsweetened, shredded coconut
- 5 beets, peeled and diced
- 1 teaspoon coarse sea salt
- 1½ cups water

INSTRUCTIONS:
a) Heat the oil in a heavy pan over medium heat.

b) Add the mustard seeds and cook for 30 seconds, or until they sizzle.

c) Add the onion and cook for 1 minute, or until it begins to brown.

d) Add the cumin, coriander, South Indian masala, and coconut.

e) Cook for 1 minute after adding the beets.

f) Add the salt and water.

g) Bring to a boil, then reduce to low heat, cover, and leave to simmer for 15 minutes.

Makes: 6 to 8 Servings

INGREDIENTS:
- 3 pounds diced beets
- 1 small red onion
- ¼ cup coconut oil
- 1 ½ teaspoon kosher salt
- ¼ teaspoon freshly ground black pepper
- 2 tablespoons rosemary leaves, chopped

INSTRUCTIONS:

a) Arrange a rack in the middle of the oven and heat the oven to 425°F.

b) Place the root vegetables and red onion on a rimmed baking sheet. Drizzle with ¼ cup coconut oil, sprinkle with kosher salt and black pepper and toss to evenly coat. Spread out in an even layer.

c) Roast for 30 minutes.

d) Remove the baking sheet from the oven, sprinkle the vegetables with the rosemary, and toss to combine. Spread back out in an even layer.

e) Continue to roast until the vegetables are tender and caramelized, 10 to 15 minutes more.

77. Beets in grand Marnier

Makes: 6 servings

INGREDIENTS:

- 6 Beets, scrubbed and trimmed
- 2 tablespoons Sweet butter
- 3 tablespoons Grand Marnier
- 1 teaspoon Grated orange rind

INSTRUCTIONS:

a) In a steamer set over simmering water, steam the beets, covered, for 25 to 35 minutes, or until they are just tender.

b) Refresh the beets under cold water, slip off the skins, and cut the beets into ⅜-inch wedges.

c) In a large skillet, cook the beets in the butter over moderate heat, stirring for 3 minutes.

d) Stir in the Grand Marnier, the orange rind, and salt to taste; simmer the mixture, covered, for 3 minutes.

78. Beets in sour cream

Makes: 4 Servings

INGREDIENTS:

- 16 ounces Can beets, drained and diced
- 1 tablespoon Cider vinegar
- ¼ teaspoon Each garlic salt and pepper
- ¼ cup Sour cream
- 1 teaspoon Sugar

INSTRUCTIONS:

a) Combine all ingredients in 1 qt glass casserole. Stir gently to mix.

b) Microwave, covered, 3-5 minutes on High, or until heated through. Stir every 2 minutes.

c) Let stand, covered, for 2-3 minutes before serving.

79. Cranberry beets

Makes: 6 Servings

INGREDIENTS:

- 1 can (16 oz.) diced beets, drained
- 1 can (16 oz.) whole berry or jellied cranberry sauce
- 2 tablespoons Orange juice
- 1 teaspoon Grated orange rind
- 1 dash Salt

INSTRUCTIONS:

a) Combine all ingredients in a saucepan; heat thoroughly, stirring occasionally.

b) Serve at once. Delicious with turkey or ham.

80. Honeyed beets

Makes: 7 servings

INGREDIENTS:
- 6 cups Water
- 1 tablespoon Vinegar
- 1 teaspoon Salt
- 5 medium Beets
- 1 medium Onion, chopped
- 2 tablespoons Margarine
- 2 tablespoons Honey
- 1 tablespoon Lemon juice
- ½ teaspoon Salt
- ⅛ teaspoon Ground cinnamon
- 1 tablespoon Parsley, snipped

INSTRUCTIONS:

a) Heat water, vinegar, and 1 teaspoon salt to boiling. Add beets. Simmer until tender, 35 to 45 minutes; drain. Run cold water over beets; slip off skins and remove root ends. Cut beets into shoestring pieces.

b) Cook and stir onion in margarine in a 10" skillet over medium heat until onion is tender about 5 minutes. Stir in beets, honey, lemon juice, ½ teaspoon salt, and cinnamon.

c) Heat stirring occasionally, until beets are hot, about 5 minutes.

d) Sprinkle with parsley.

81. Roasted Beet Wedges

Makes: 4

INGREDIENTS:
- 1-pound medium fresh beets, peeled
- 1/2 teaspoon kosher salt
- 8 teaspoons vegetable broth
- 5 fresh rosemary sprigs

INSTRUCTIONS:
a) Preheat the oven to 400 °F.
b) Cut each beet into wedges depending on how many servings are desired. Toss in the vegetable broth and salt to coat.
c) In a baking pan, place a 12-inch-long piece of heavy-duty foil.
d) Arrange the beets on the foil and sprinkle with rosemary. Wrap the beets in foil and seal tightly.
e) Bake for at least 1 hour or until the potatoes are tender.
f) Allow the steam to escape by carefully opening the foil. Remove the rosemary sprigs. Serve and enjoy!

SAUCES AND RELISHES

82. Beet Marmalade

Makes: 2 jars

INGREDIENTS:
- 4 red beets, roasted and peeled
- 1 ½ cups sugar
- 1 lemon
- 2 tablespoons ginger, chopped

INSTRUCTIONS:
a) Firstly, trim down the stalks and remove the thin root end.
b) Wrap the beet with foil and put it onto the baking sheet. Place it into the oven and cook for 45 Minutes to 1 minute. Let it cool, and then peel it.
c) Add beet to the food processor and pulse until chopped.
d) Transfer the beets to the saucepan. Then, add sugar and stir well.
e) Cut the lemon into big chunks and add it into the food processor with chopped ginger. Blend until smooth.
f) Place it into the saucepan and cook on medium-low heat.
g) Place hot marmalade into the hot and sterilized jars, leaving ¼-inch headspace.
h) Add water into the water bath canner and bring to a boil.
i) Place jars into the water bath canner and bring to a boil.
j) Cover the water bath canner and process for 15 Minutes.
k) Remove the jars from the water bath canner and cool them.

83. Beetroot Relish

Makes: 2 jars

INGREDIENTS:
- Beetroot, 2 cups
- Oranges, 2
- Apple cider vinegar, 500ml
- Brown sugar, 400g
- Onions, 3, chopped
- Apples, 3, peeled and chopped
- Garlic, 2 cloves, crushed
- Salt, 1 tablespoon
- Cloves, 4
- Bay leaf, 1
- Cinnamon, 1 stick
- Fresh ginger, 1 teaspoon, grated
- Chili, 2, chopped

INSTRUCTIONS:
a) Add all ingredients to the pot and simmer for 1 hour.
b) Discard bay leaf and cinnamon stick.
c) When done, transfer the mixture to the jars, leaving ¼-inch headspace.
d) Place the jars into the water bath canner.
e) Process for 5 Minutes.
f) Keep it for up to a month in the fridge.

INGREDIENTS:
- 8 small beets
- 1 cup cider vinegar
- 1 teaspoon salt
- ¼ cup sugar
- 5 peppercorns
- 1 teaspoon pickling spice
- 1 bay leaf, fresh drill

INSTRUCTIONS:
a) Cook beets somewhat firm.
b) Drain reserving 1 cup of liquid.
c) Fill a jar to about ¼ inch from the top
d) Combine the beet liquid with the rest of the liquid and spices and bring to a boil, fill jar, and process for 10 minutes.

DESSERT

85. Beet-lime ganache

Makes: 1½ Cups

INGREDIENTS:
- 2 medium beets, peeled and cut into chunks
- 1 lime
- milk if needed
- 4¼ ounces white chocolate
- 2 tablespoons butter
- ¼ cup glucose
- ¼ cup cold heavy cream
- ¾ teaspoon kosher salt

INSTRUCTIONS:
a) Heat the oven to 325°F.

b) Wrap the beet chunks up in a big sheet of aluminum foil and put them on a sheet pan for easy handling. Roast for 1 to 2 hours, or until the beets are on the mushy side of tender; give them additional 30-minute intervals in the oven if they aren't.

c) Meanwhile, grate the zest from the lime; reserve. Squeeze 8 g (2 teaspoons) juice from the lime and reserve.

d) Transfer the beets to a blender and puree them. (If your blender is giving you trouble, add up to 1 tablespoon of milk to help get it going.) Pass the puree through a fine-mesh strainer—it should have the texture of Libby's pumpkin puree (or baby food). Measure out 120 g (⅓ cup) beet puree. Let cool.

e) Combine the white chocolate and butter in a microwave-safe dish and gently melt them in the microwave in 15-second bursts, stirring between blasts. The result should be barely warm to the touch and homogenous.

f) Transfer the chocolate mixture to a container that can accommodate an immersion blender—something tall and narrow, like a 1-quart plastic deli container. Warm the glucose in the microwave for 15 seconds, then immediately add it to the chocolate mixture and buzz with the hand blender. After a minute, stream in the heavy cream, with the hand blender running—the mixture will come together into something silky, shiny, and smooth.

g) Blend in the beet puree, lime zest, and salt. Put the ganache in the fridge for 30 minutes to firm up.

h) Use a spatula to fold the lime juice into the ganache (do not do this until the ganache is set, or you will break the ganache). Put the ganache back in the fridge for at least 3 hours, or, ideally, overnight. Stored in an airtight container, it will keep in the fridge for 1 week. Serve cold.

86. Beet cake

Makes: 10 Servings

INGREDIENTS:
- 1 cup Crisco oil
- ½ cup butter, melted
- 3 eggs
- 2 cup sugar
- 2½ cup flour
- 2 teaspoons cinnamon
- 2 teaspoons baking soda
- 1 teaspoon salt
- 2 teaspoons vanilla
- 1 cup Harvard beets
- ½ cup creamed cottage cheese
- 1 cup crushed pineapple, drained
- 1 cup chopped nuts
- ½ cup coconut

INSTRUCTIONS:
a) Mix oil, butter, eggs, and sugar.

b) Add in flour, cinnamon, soda, and salt.

c) Fold in vanilla, beets, cottage cheese, pineapple, nuts, and coconut.

d) Pour into a 9x13-inch pan.

e) Bake at 350 for 40-45 minutes. Serve with whipped cream.

Makes: 4 servings

INGREDIENTS:

- 4 cups Sliced beets (both red and Yellow), sliced ½-inch Thick
- 1 cup Thinly-sliced onions
- 2 cups Seasoned bread crumbs
- 3 tablespoons Butter
- Olive oil, for drizzling
- Parmesan cheese, for Sprinkling
- Creole seasoning, for Sprinkling
- Salt and white pepper

INSTRUCTIONS:

a) Preheat oven to 375 degrees F. In a buttered gratin or heavy baking dish, layer beets, onions, and half of the bread crumbs dotting each with butter and seasoning each layer with olive oil, Parmesan cheese, Creole seasoning, and salt and pepper, to taste.
b) Finish with bread crumb layer on top. Bake, covered, for 45 minutes. Uncover and continue baking for 15 minutes more, or until the top is browned and bubbly. Serve directly from the dish.

88. Beet green souffle

Makes: 1 souffle

INGREDIENTS:
- 3 tablespoons Parmesan cheese; grated
- 2 mediums Beets; cooked and peeled
- 2 tablespoons Butter
- 2 tablespoons Flour
- ¾ cup Chicken broth; hot
- 1 cup Beet greens; sauteed
- ½ cup Cheddar cheese; grated
- 3 Egg yolks
- 4 Egg whites

INSTRUCTIONS:
a) Butter a 1 qt. souffle dish; sprinkle with Parmesan cheese. Slice the cooked beets and line the bottom of the souffle dish with them.
b) In a small saucepan, melt the butter, stir in the flour, add the hot broth and continue to cook until slightly thickened, then transfer to a larger bowl. Coarsely chop beet greens and add to the sauce along with Cheddar cheese.
c) In a separate bowl, beat egg yolks; blend them with beet green mixture. Beat egg whites until they form peaks. Fold into a bowl with other ingredients; blend well. Transfer all to a buttered souffle dish. Sprinkle with Parmesan cheese.
d) Bake at 350 F. for 30 minutes, or until the souffle is puffed and golden.

89. Beet mousse

Makes: 1 Serving

INGREDIENTS:
- 3 mediums Beets; Cooked on their skin
- 2½ cup Chicken broth
- 2 packs of Unflavored gelatin
- 1 cup Unflavored yogurt
- 2 tablespoons Lemon or lime juice
- 1 small Grated onion
- 1 tablespoon Sugar
- 1 tablespoon Mustard
- Salt and pepper; to taste

INSTRUCTIONS:
a) Peel and cube-cooked beets.
b) Place gelatin in a bowl with 6 T water, and stir. Let stand for 2 minutes and pour hot chicken stock stirring.
c) Process together all the ingredients except gelatin. Correct seasoning.
d) Add cooled gelatin and process just to blend.
e) Pour into an oiled mold to set 6. Unmold and serve in the center of the plate surrounded by chicken curry salad or shrimp salad

90. Beet nut bread

Makes: 1 serving

INGREDIENTS:
- ¾ cup Shortening
- 1 cup Sugar
- 4 Eggs
- 2 teaspoons Vanilla
- 2 cups Shredded beets
- 3 cups Flour
- 2 teaspoons Baking powder
- 1 teaspoon Baking soda
- ½ teaspoon Cinnamon
- ¼ teaspoon Ground nutmeg
- 1 cup Chopped nuts

INSTRUCTIONS:
a) Beat shortening and sugar until light and fluffy. Blend in eggs and vanilla. Stir in beets.

b) Add combined dry ingredients; mix well. Stir in nuts.

c) Pour into greased and floured 9x5" loaf pan.

d) Bake at 350'F. for 60-70 minutes or until the wooden toothpick inserted in the center comes out clean.

e) Cool for 10 minutes; remove from pan.

91. Roasted Beet and Goat Cheese Tart

Ingredients:

1 sheet puff pastry, thawed
2 large beets, roasted and sliced
4 oz goat cheese, crumbled
1/4 cup chopped walnuts
2 tbsp honey
2 tbsp balsamic vinegar
2 tbsp olive oil
Salt and pepper, to taste
Instructions:

Preheat the oven to 375°F (190°C).

Roll out the puff pastry on a lightly floured surface.

Transfer the puff pastry to a baking sheet.

Arrange the roasted and sliced beets on top of the puff pastry.

Sprinkle the crumbled goat cheese and chopped walnuts on top of the beets.

Drizzle the honey, balsamic vinegar, and olive oil on top of the tart.

Season with salt and pepper, to taste.

Bake for 25-30 minutes or until the pastry is golden brown.

Serve warm.

92. Beet and Feta Tart

Ingredients:

1 store-bought pie crust
2 large beets, roasted and sliced
1/2 cup crumbled feta cheese
1/4 cup chopped fresh parsley
2 eggs
1/2 cup heavy cream
Salt and pepper, to taste
Instructions:

Preheat the oven to 375°F (190°C).

Roll out the pie crust and transfer it to a 9-inch (23 cm) tart pan.

Arrange the roasted and sliced beets on top of the pie crust.

Sprinkle the crumbled feta cheese and chopped fresh parsley on top.

In a separate small mixing bowl, whisk together the eggs and heavy cream.

Pour the egg mixture over the beet and feta mixture.

Season with salt and pepper, to taste.

Bake in the preheated oven for 30-35 minutes, or until the tart is set and the crust is golden brown.

Serve warm or at room temperature.

DRINKS

93. Cucumber beetroot drink

Makes: 2

INGREDIENTS:
- 3 carrots
- 1 cucumber
- 1 green pepper
- 1 beetroot (medium)
- 2 tomatoes
- 1 inch of ginger

INSTRUCTIONS:
a) Thoroughly wash and coarsely cut all components.
b) Juice everything except the cucumber, which you'll juice after the ginger to get everything through the juicer.

Makes: 2

INGREDIENTS:

- 1 cup frozen strawberries, peeled and sliced
- 1 beetroot, peeled and chopped
- 1 cup apple, peeled, cored, and sliced
- 3 Medjool dates, pitted and chopped
- ¼ cup extra-virgin coconut oil
- ½ cup almond milk, unsweetened

INSTRUCTIONS:

a) Combine all ingredients and blend until smooth.

b) Pour the smoothie into two glasses and serve.

95. Beet Juice with Ginger and Lemon

Ingredients:

2 medium beets, peeled and chopped
1 inch piece of fresh ginger, peeled and chopped
1 lemon, juiced
1-2 cups of water
Instructions:

Add the beets, ginger, and lemon juice to a blender.

Add enough water to cover the ingredients.

Blend until smooth.

Strain through a fine mesh strainer or cheesecloth.

Serve over ice.

96. Beet and Pineapple Smoothie

Ingredients:

2 medium beets, peeled and chopped
1 cup frozen pineapple chunks
1 banana
1 cup coconut water
1 tbsp honey
Instructions:

Add the beets, pineapple chunks, banana, coconut water, and honey to a blender.

Blend until smooth.

Serve over ice.

97. Beet and Berry Smoothie

Ingredients:

2 medium beets, peeled and chopped
1 cup mixed berries (strawberries, blueberries, raspberries)
1 banana
1 cup almond milk
1 tbsp honey
Instructions:

Add the beets, mixed berries, banana, almond milk, and honey to a blender.

Blend until smooth.

Serve over ice.

98. Beet and Carrot Juice

Ingredients:

2 medium beets, peeled and chopped
2 medium carrots, peeled and chopped
1 apple, cored and chopped
1 inch piece of fresh ginger, peeled and chopped
Instructions:

Add the beets, carrots, apple, and ginger to a juicer.

Juice the ingredients.

Serve over ice.

99. Beet Kvass

Ingredients:

2 medium beets, peeled and chopped
1 tbsp sea salt
4 cups filtered water
Instructions:

Add the beets, sea salt, and filtered water to a glass jar.
Cover the jar with a lid and shake to dissolve the salt.
Leave the jar at room temperature for 2-3 days, or until the
mixture turns slightly sour and bubbly.
Strain the mixture through a fine mesh strainer.
Serve the kvass chilled.

CONCLUSION

We hope that this cookbook has given you a newfound appreciation for the humble beet and all the delicious ways it can be used in the kitchen. Whether you're looking for healthy, nutrient-packed meals or simply want to add some vibrant color to your dishes, beets are a versatile and delicious option.

By incorporating beets into your cooking, you can take advantage of their numerous health benefits, from boosting your immune system to improving your athletic performance. So, don't be afraid to experiment with different recipes and cooking techniques, and discover the endless possibilities of this amazing root vegetable.

Thank you for choosing our Beet Cookbook, and we hope that the recipes and tips provided in this book will inspire you to make beets a regular part of your diet. Happy cooking!

Milton Keynes UK
Ingram Content Group UK Ltd.
UKHW022025170823
427026UK00016B/661